To: _____

From: _____

Published by Sellers Publishing, Inc.
Text and illustrations copyright © 2013 Sandy Gingras

Sellers Publishing, Inc.
161 John Roberts Road, South Portland, Maine 04106
Visit our Web site: www.sellerspublishing.com
E-mail: rsp@rsvp.com

ISBN 13: 978-1-4162-0891-4

10 9 8 7 6 5 4 3

Printed and bound in China.

I believe in you

by Sandy Gingras

SELLERS
PUBLISHING

This book is for you...
because
I want you to know that
I believe in your spirit
and your heart and your
talents. No matter what
life brings, you can
trust to this: I
believe in
you.

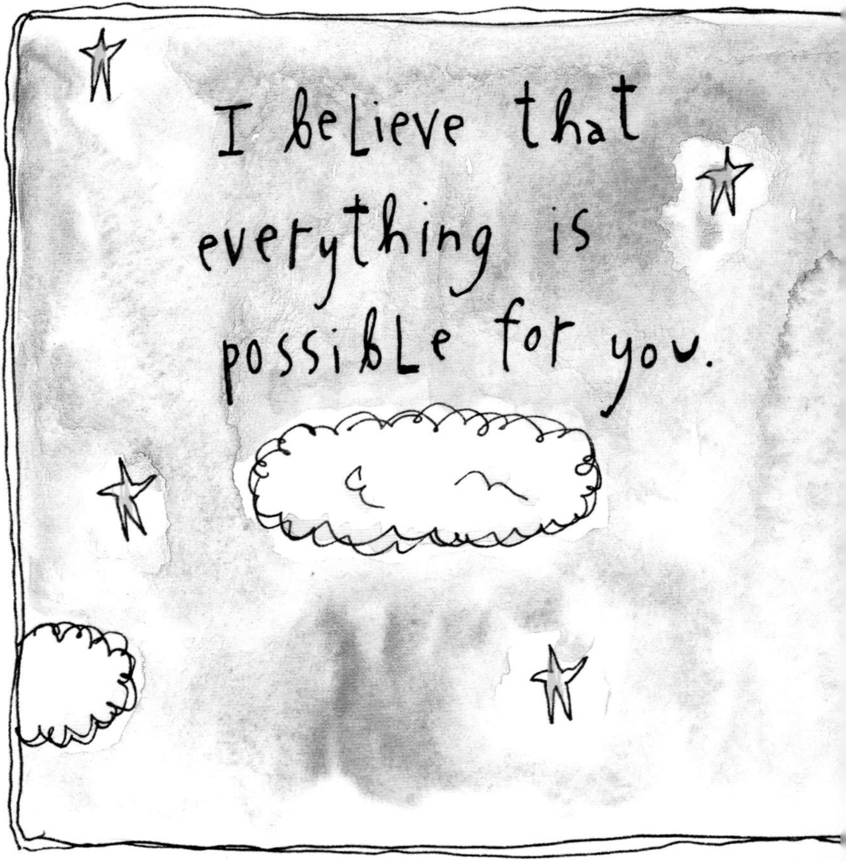
I believe that
everything is
possible for you.

I believe in following your heart.

I beLieve
you can go far.

I believe in doing what makes you feel most alive.

I believe that the recipe for success always involves adding Love...

I believe in

being carried
away by your
dreams.

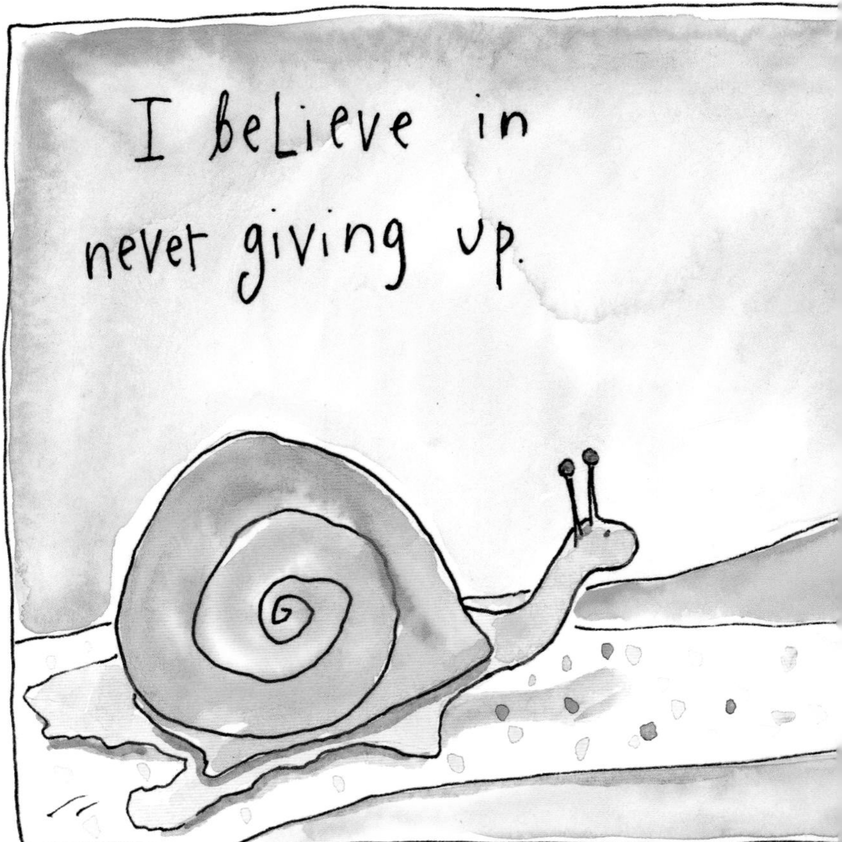
I believe in never giving up.

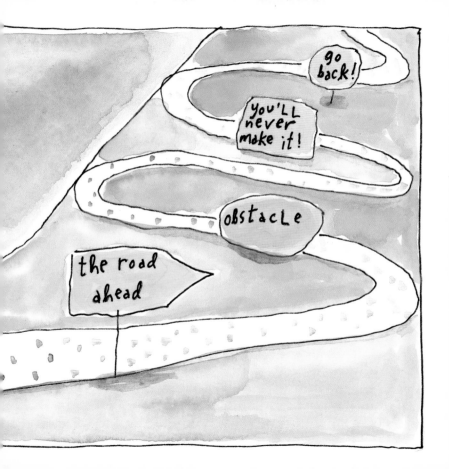

Standing
tall
and
proud.
(even when you're
feeling small)

I believe in
letting go
of control, and

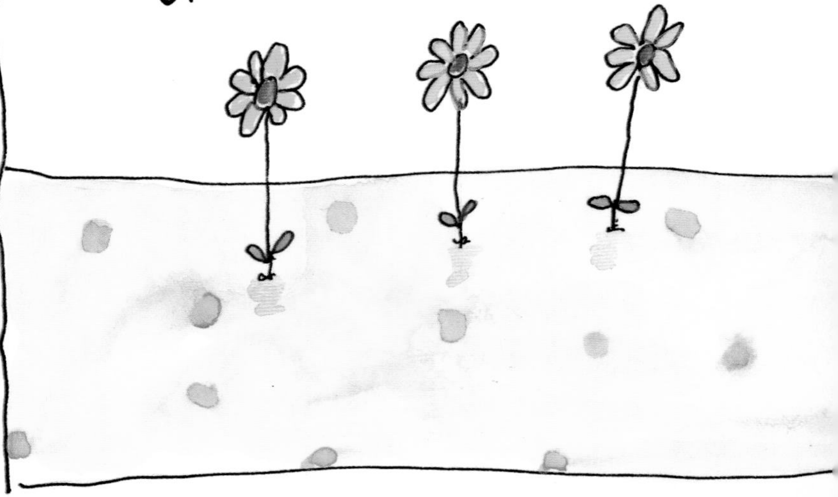

trusting yourself.

I believe in you.

I believe in
throwing off
your Lines,
LiFE:
corporate
headquarters

and
sailing away
from safety.

I believe that
the opposite of Life
is fear.

I can
fly
if I give
myself
a chance
but if I
stay within
myself, I'll
never Know
about the
sun on
my face
and the
wind

LIVING

today,

not

Tomorrow

I believe that,

"Life is not about finding yourself,

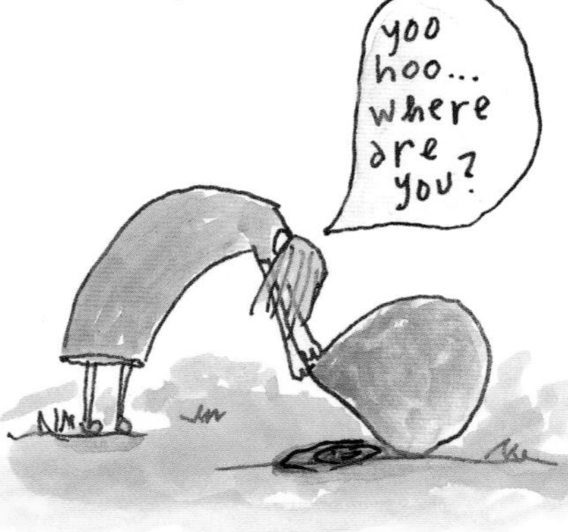

it's about

creating yourself."

—George Bernard Shaw

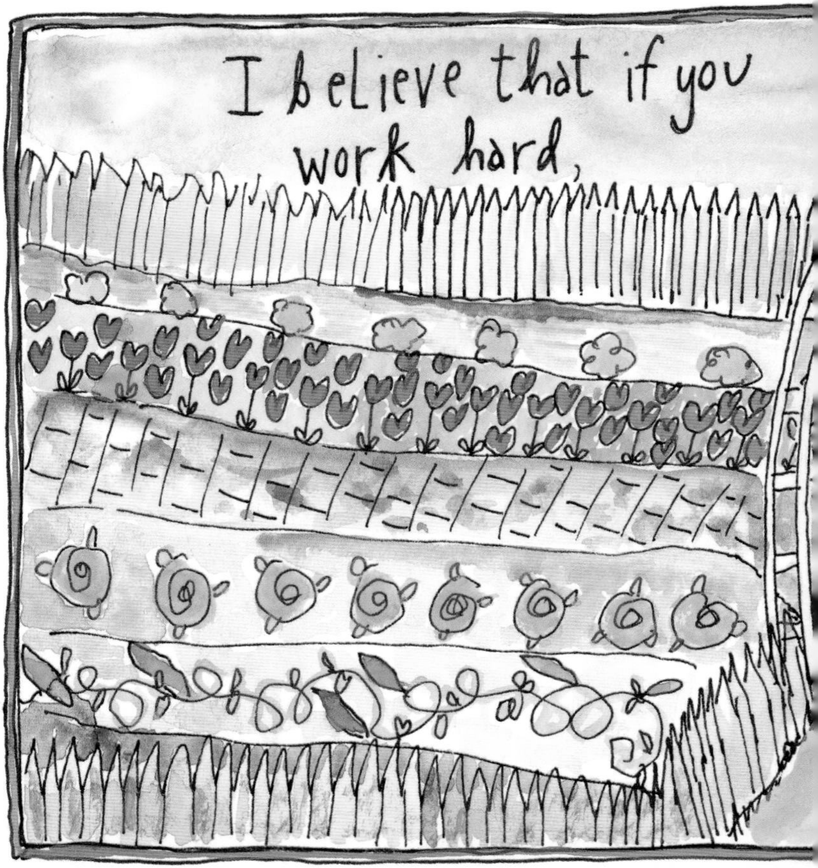

I beLieve in

ACCËNTUATING

the
positive.

nd enthusiastic. zesty. full of

nd brave. full of vi

growing and

hoping and -

and lau along

nd wishing on st

dream and dream

and all the moment

knowing that you have

up intuiting an sprouting an

and it is just a big adventure

mistakes and laugh at yourself. and

I beLieve in
Living with
passion.

lots of verve. fired up. feisty and vinegar. jumping in. risking yourself being afraid to change f possibility way. dance never being are. celebrate your life. sp 85. blossoming ating and express ive in and splash in the process and be la nights and tra la la days and

I beLieve in Loving your Life.

exploring and giggl afraid to yourself reading and opening and exploring around and make on a journey of

I believe that you are always stronger than you think you are.

I believe in you.

I believe in leaving your comfort zone.

I believe in going for it.

I beLieve in

trusting the journey,

not the road's end.

I believe
in making
your own path.

I believe that we never stop growing.

I believe that mistakes make us wiser, and obstacles make us stronger.

knocked down, but getting up again...

I believe that, if you live thankfully, your life will fill with abundance.

I believe that you can make

I believe in you.